Emu

by Grace Hansen

Abdo Kids Jumbo is an Imprint of Abdo Kids
abdobooks.com

abdobooks.com

Published by Abdo Kids, a division of ABDO, P.O. Box 398166, Minneapolis, Minnesota 55439.
Copyright © 2020 by Abdo Consulting Group, Inc. International copyrights reserved in all countries.
No part of this book may be reproduced in any form without written permission from the publisher.
Abdo Kids Jumbo™ is a trademark and logo of Abdo Kids.

Printed in the United States of America, North Mankato, Minnesota.

052019

092019

 THIS BOOK CONTAINS RECYCLED MATERIALS

Photo Credits: Alamy, iStock, Shutterstock, SuperStock

Production Contributors: Teddy Borth, Jennie Forsberg, Grace Hansen
Design Contributors: Dorothy Toth, Pakou Moua

Library of Congress Control Number: 2018963333
Publisher's Cataloging-in-Publication Data

Names: Hansen, Grace, author.
Title: Emu / by Grace Hansen.
Description: Minneapolis, Minnesota : Abdo Kids, 2020 | Series: Australian
    animals | Includes online resources and index.
Identifiers: ISBN 9781532185434 (lib. bdg.) | ISBN 9781532186417 (ebook) |
    ISBN 9781532186905 (Read-to-me ebook)
Subjects: LCSH: Emus--Juvenile literature. | Birds--Australia--Identification--
    Juvenile literature. | Animals--Australia--Juvenile literature.
Classification: DDC 598.524--dc23

Table of Contents

Emus

Emus live throughout Australia. They are the second-largest bird in the world. They can grow to be 6.2 feet (1.89 m) tall!

Though they have wings and feathers, they are flightless. Their tiny wings are useless to their large bodies.

An emu's feathers hang loosely from its body. The feathers look more like hair because of the way they grow.

9

Emus make up for their **inability** to fly by being fast! They can run up to 30 miles per hour (48.28 km/h).

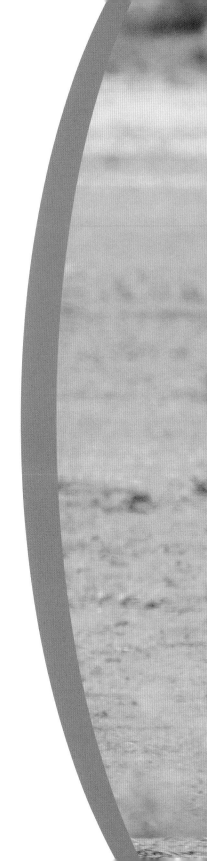

Their long, powerful legs help them jump 7 feet (2.13 m) high! They use their heavy feet and nails to fight.

Flocks & Food

Emus **migrate** to find food and water. They do this as a group called a flock. Flocks can be found in forests, woodlands, and desert shrublands.

An emu's diet changes with the seasons. In the springtime, there are lots of grasshoppers and fruits to eat. During the rainy season, they feast on grass shoots and caterpillars.

Their beaks are wide and pointed. This shape helps emus graze on plants.

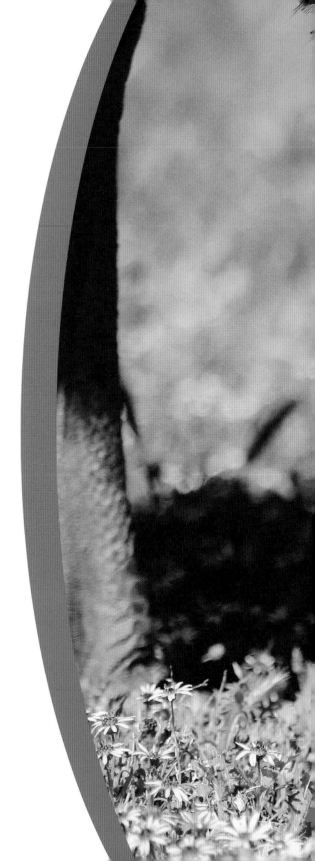

Babies

A female emu lays 5 to 15 eggs at a time. She might lay eggs three times each year. The eggs hatch after about 8 weeks. Baby emus can walk soon after hatching.

More Facts

- Emus are the second-largest bird.
  Ostriches are the first.

- Wild emus live between 10 and 20 years.
  In captivity, they can live up to 35 years!

- Emus are good swimmers.

Glossary

graze – to feed on growing grass.

inability – lack of ability to do something.

migrate – to move from one region into another.

Index

Abdo Kids
ONLINE
FREE! ONLINE MULTIMEDIA RESOURCES

Visit **abdokids.com** to access crafts, games, videos, and more!

Use Abdo Kids code

AEK5434

or scan this QR code!